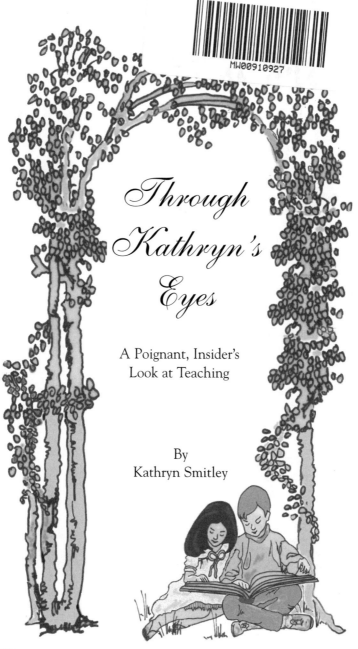

Through Kathryn's Eyes

A Poignant, Insider's
Look at Teaching

By
Kathryn Smitley

"Different" Books
From The Place in the Woods
Golden Valley, Minnesota USA

This is another **A++** book from **The Place in the Woods**.

Design and layout by Deborah Truscott
Illustrations by Kathryn Smitley and Deborah Truscott

Consultants: Diane Barish, Janny Davis Boyce, David and Susan George, Diane Jenkins, Janice Shaffer and Sally Todd

Cover: Kathryn Panich Smitley as a child

The author's nephew, Keith George, appears on page 105

LIBRARY OF CONGRESS CATALOGING-IN-PUBLICATION DATA

Smitley, Kathryn, 1949-
    Through Kathryn's eyes : a poignant, insider's look at teaching / Kathryn A. Smitley.
        p.   cm.
    ISBN 0-932991-32-7
    1. Autistic children—Education Poetry. 2. Special education teachers Poetry. 3. Teaching Poetry.   I. Title
PS3569.M58T47   1999   99-36614
811'.54—dc21   CIP

| THROUGH KATHRYN'S EYES | ISBN |
| *A Poignant, Insider's Look at Teaching* | 0-932991-32-7 |

First Printing September 1999
© The Place in the Woods

"Different" Books is an imprint of
The Place in the Woods
3900 Glenwood Avenue
Golden Valley, MN 55422-5302

OTHER TITLES FROM THE PLACE IN THE WOODS INCLUDE:

	ISBN
(Children's Fiction)	
The Flying Frog Circus	0-932991-61-0
Simon the Daredevil Centipede	0-932991-58-0
Little Horse	0-932991-59-9
(Adult non-fiction)	
African America: Heralding the Heritage	0-932991-05-x
American Woman: Hidden in History, Forging the Future	0-932991-27-0
Hispanic America: Freeing the Free, Honoring Heroes	0-932991-04-1
The People: Native Americans— Thoughts and Feelings	0-932991-03-3
"My Own Book!"—A History of RIF	0-932991-50-5

This book is dedicated to three in Heaven
and one on Earth

Table of Contents

Acknowledgments

When a book has been completed it is difficult to acknowledge all the people who helped make it happen. To the many fine people who offered support, I thank you. It was your encouragement which allowed me the confidence to keep writing.

Yet there are specific people who must be recognized for their contributions.

To my childhood friend, John Taylor, who, since high school, believed that I had something worthwhile to say and therefore kept the small flame of hope alive—I thank you. Your faith in me means everything.

To the children who come through the schoolhouse door year after year, delighting, captivating and encouraging my thought—I thank you. My relationship with you brings me wisdom.

To my friends and teaching colleagues who inspire, listen and share my joy—I thank you. Your encouragement keeps me writing.

To Diane Jenkins, a wonderful friend who encouraged, loved and listened to my poems from the beginning—I thank you. Your enthusiasm gives me confidence.

To Mohamoud Mohamed, my friend who has shared the classroom with me for many years and has always listened, laughed and encouraged me to write—I thank you. Your kind spirit fosters a warm sense of family in our classroom.

To my principal, Shirley McCoy, who delighted in and saved my poems in a special file—I thank you. Your approval allows me to trust myself.

To my publisher, Roger Hammer, whose wisdom inspired me to write many of the poetic snapshots—I thank you. You knew what I could do before I did.

To Debbie Truscott, my dear friend since college, who devoted her time, attention and patience to polish the imagery and presentation of each poem—I thank you. I depend upon your skill and talent and you are always faithful.

To my friend, Linda Thrasher, who is also a special education teacher and who gave the manuscript a teacher's seal of approval—I thank you. Your opinion validates mine.

To my dear friends Janice and George Shaffer, who were with me where it all began back in the days of the Masai Indians—I thank you. You know what I mean.

To my wonderful extended family whose creativity and humor both delight my imagination and provide me with a secure place in this world—I thank you. We even made a place for "Nasty Grover!"

To my David, the master builder who provided me with a lovely home from which to write—I thank you. The beauty of your handiwork always gives me comfort.

To Jeanette, who nudged me in the right direction—I thank you. You were the catalyst who helped to make it happen.

To Sue Bell, the Cabaret Girl and master chef who, once upon a time, nurtured us all—I thank you...wherever you are.

And to you, Mary and Tom Panich, my wonderful parents whose lives of integrity inspired me—I thank you. May God bless you always.

K.S.

Foreword

Teachers are a very special breed.

They take our children into their classrooms, almost like immigrants from a foreign land, and feed and clothe them with knowledge for their journey through life.

I have two aunts who were teachers. Aunt Elizabeth had two children of her own. Aunt Gertrude had none, but went through life making students her "love adopted" children. She nurtures and loves them as deeply as any parent, even today in her eighties. Teachers from my high school years still keep contact and interest in my journey.

Among special education challenges, one of the greatest is the field of autism where children often have withdrawn to live in a world of their own where they feel safe.

When I first met Kathryn, she had written some poems and wanted to see if they were publishable. I encountered a double whammy. Her poems had a wonderful touch and insight. And as I talked to her, as I looked into her eyes, I became aware that her presence had virtually slipped inside me and was poking around to see what was going on. It was an eerie feeling, but I realized it was probably what she did with her children. She didn't just work outside them, but inside them as well.

So it came as no surprise, when Kathryn told me stories of her children, to learn how her students had blossomed. There was the little boy who wasn't talking when he came to school in September, but by June he had a featured role in the school talent show. Another child terrorized teachers with his temper tantrums, yet after weeks with Kathryn he was beginning to sit quietly and began bringing her purse to her when it was time to go to lunch.

In her first book, Kathryn, who holds a Bachelor of Fine Arts from Old Dominion University and a Master's in Education from George Mason University, celebrates teaching and working with autistic children. Her unusual insight is based on more than 20 years of teaching. You will have the rare experience of seeing "Through Kathryn's Eyes" how one very special teacher "sees the child, nurtures the hope."

Roger A. Hammer, author

African America
American Woman
The People
Hispanic America
"My Own Book!"

Dear Reader,

My mind compels me to write this book as my way of sharing what I have come to know, love and enjoy.

As a young child I was introduced to teaching as I watched the play "The Miracle Worker." The realization that Anne Sullivan made Helen Keller achieve a level of understanding in the face of tremendous odds, was awe-inspiring.

Throughout college I enjoyed writing and always kept a personal journal. I was intrigued with the meaning of the word "understand," and once wrote it on a wooden post on the campus during the late sixties—a time of much turmoil. Only later as a teacher would I come to feel the impact of that word.

When I went back to college for my master's degree in education, the word "understand" was again emphasized. One of my professors, Dr. Barbara Given, once stated in class that as a special education teacher it would be my job to make children understand, and that I could do whatever I had to, within reason, to achieve this end. I carried her permission with me feeling that it somehow gave me authorization to pursue avenues which other teachers might have overlooked. In fact, I still keep it handy, just in case! However, at the time she made this statement I had no idea what I would do; yet I knew I'd do it and I have.

For me it is important to be an agent for good, so to that end I am committed. I know I have made mistakes, hopefully not too many, but my intentions are honorable and I seek always to help. On the path of education I wish to regard myself as a stepping stone, not a stumbling block.

This book is my way of allowing you, the reader, to step into the world of special education, which I have embraced for more than twenty years. My hope is that as you journey through these poems you will feel joy and compassion, experience laughter and indignation, and be touched by the profound differences that define lives previously not fully understood.

I also hope these poems inspire us to begin thinking in ways that broaden our awareness and offer possibilities that enable the circle of education to be drawn larger, providing a comfortable place for each child, including those with disabilities.

Kathryn

How It All Began....

Empathy

As a tiny child I sat long ago,
   Watching Beauty and The Beast.
I observed it all with wonderment—
There was much on which to feast.

The plight of the Beast was miserable,
Condemned to a life of despair.
Beauty was the only joy he had,
As long as she remained in his care.

But his grief was overwhelming,
Bringing many tears to my eyes.
And even though I seemed terribly sad,
I would not admit that I cried.

So when questioned by my mother,
Who saw on my face a slight frown,
I simply replied, "I not crying,
But my tears are dwipping down."

And so they've continued their
      downward descent—
I always feel what I see.
My empathy began as a tiny child
As I sat on my mother's knee.

Mother Dear

What is taught to children
    From one generation to another?
How is it transmitted?
Is it passed down from our mothers?

What did I really learn from you
When I was just a baby?
Did you teach me about a guiding force?
Well, perhaps you did—just maybe!

We were outside one summer day
Playing with a snake so small.
But it slithered off in a hurry
And was gone in grass quite tall.

I cried to have the snake return,
So you offered a silent request.
By asking God to bring it back
You put your faith to the test.

In time you felt a cool silky touch...
The snake slid over your hand.
You were filled with a sense of abiding strength—
It came from an essence quite grand.

As you walked into our tiny house
This essence stayed strong.
It lingered throughout the rest of the day,
And remained all night long.

It comforted you with its presence,
Allowed you to truly know,
That your faith is terribly important—
It's vital you not let it go!

And I want you to know this, Mother—
That my faith was also made clear.
He spoke to me while in your arms–
He did this through you, Mother Dear!

Heaven Knows

As a young child
To a theatre I was taken.
I saw a remarkable performance—
My spirit was awakened.

Upon the stage I witnessed
A miracle taking place:
Anne Sullivan's powerful teaching
Lit Helen Keller's face.

She did this with courage
And the strength of her mighty will.
She sought out Helen's spirit,
With love and a teacher's skill.

Did seeing this have a profound effect
On the profession that I choose?
I would guess it probably did—
But only Heaven knows!

Years and years have passed, but still
Anne's spirit talks to me.
In class she reaches the children I teach...
Who are no longer blind—but now see.

What It Means to be a Teacher....

The Job

I'm just a teacher,
    That's who I am.
I'm roasted each day
Like a fat Christmas ham.

Cut and sliced
And ready to serve,
I'm dead in this job
With not one living nerve.

Commitments and duties
Have taken their toll.
Meetings and schedules
Have put teaching on hold.

Deadlines and due dates,
Committees and such...
It's all overwhelming
And entirely too much!

Please allow me to teach,
It's what I do best.
I can't manage it all—
To heck with the rest!

The Process of Wisdom

*W*hat is this process so many now know,
The art of seeing into what doesn't
show?

How does it happen, where does it begin?
Is it something more common to women than men?

For a young child, what he senses is real—
He doesn't yet value an emotion he'll feel.

And even though it may touch his heart,
He's unable to see, sensing only just part.

Yet, when the senses are full, his mind has a need
To question the knowledge, examine the deed—

To look close inside at the soul deep within,
Kept in abeyance from the eyes of most men.

So as a child watches, but doesn't yet know—
He'll sense part of a truth by all that will show.

But he fails to see all that is real—
To understand, a person must feel.

It is then that real wisdom can come to your heart.
Through unspoken knowledge which your mind
will impart.

My Family

I live in a house,
    But I'm mostly alone,
So I spend many evenings
With friends on the phone.

I haven't a family,
No children of mine—
Just a small class of boys
Who take all of my time.

We feel like a family,
A large bundle of joy.
I cherish the essence
Of each little boy.

They trust in me
And await each day,
For the guidance I offer,
And the things that I say.

Like baby birds
Who yearn for the sky,
My family of boys
Want only to try.

I give to each child
What I believe he needs,
To promote his knowledge
Of thought, word and deed.

Guiding, caring,
As any mother would,
Seeking the best
As a good parent should.

But...I'm not a mother—
Or is that true?
Were you given to me
Or I to you?

To have and hold,
For a time so brief,
Your innocent love
quite softens my grief...

And offers me memories
Of sons that I've missed—
Eyes never seen,
Faces never kissed.

Sand Castles

Every day I take my place,
Upon the beach I stand.
Fashion a brand new castle
From wet chunks of gritty sand.

This building is done daily,
It's something I know how to do.
The castle represents my knowledge—
It's a gift from me to you.

But the tide surges forward
And destroys what I have made.
It does this all quite naturally,
Then back to the ocean it fades.

And not unlike the ocean,
Children, prepared to jest,
Will surge into your classroom
Bringing havoc and unrest.

They'll take your instructional castle
And level it to the ground.
Then disappear at the end of every day
In a flood of tumultuous sound.

Then it's up to you, a teacher,
To rebuild the castle again.
Up high on the beach and out of reach—
Some place where it's never been.

So that after this job is finished,
And you've checked what you have done,
Hope that your castle will weather the surge—
Prepared for the tide that will come.

Decisions, Decisions

*D*ecisions are a part of life,
　　Whether young or old.
They direct our lives in many ways—
Or so we're always told.

Decisions are the beams and boards,
Building bridges on which reside
The hopes and dreams we have in life—
Over them our journey rides.

Good decisions are sound and strong,
They'll easily hold your weight.
But bad ones have so many flaws,
They'll drop you to your fate!

Decisions will direct your life,
Of that there is no doubt.
The kind of people we become
Are what bridges are all about.

So teach your children wisely
About the choices that they make.
Help them to build bridges
That are strong and will not break.

Explain responsibility
And what decisions mean.
Let them see how broken boards
Won't take them to their dreams.

Model good decisions;
Children learn by watching you.
Then check what they do daily,
Or they're likely to fall through.

The Day Begins

Early in the morning
As I slowly wake from sleep,
I think about the day to come
And promises I must keep.

I remember jobs unfinished
And appointments not yet made.
I recall some files I've left untouched,
A few perhaps mislaid.

I question the schedule of meetings
And the agenda I've laid out.
I want each day to run smoothly—
Let laughter be about.

But uncertainty often plagues me
And keeps worry in my mind.
I question myself far too much—
Mentally, I'm in a bind.

As I lay in bed reflecting
On all that I must do,
I silently ask a blessing,
My sanity to renew—

And pray when the day is over
And a memory of mine alone,
That gladness fills my heart with hope
As I make my way back home.

Cookin'

I can't prepare a casserole,
   I'm not really much of a cook.
Anything that I attempt
Usually comes straight from a book.

But in class it's a different story—
I toss the children about,
Spicing up their hearts and minds,
In the classroom and out.

Yes, I plan the instructional menu
During mornings and after snack.
I'm never sure just what I'll fix,
But it supplements what the children lack.

I season everything with laughter,
Smiles and hugs and love.
Often, as we're dining out,
I seek guidance from above.

The meals that I prepare at school
Offer pleasure and insight.
For they feed the mind of the little child
Who's learning wrong from right!

The Risk We Take

I will try to direct your thinking
   Through images and words I say.
I'll hope they offer you guidance
And support you along your way.

But the truth is you don't listen
And you rarely follow through.
You often make bad choices
And pursue what you shouldn't do!

So this means I must find you
And acknowledge that you're lost,
Interrupt your journey to nowhere...
No matter my personal cost.

So I leave the class behind me
To form barriers which are strong,
Letting you know quite clearly
That the path you're on is wrong.

To draw you back I expose myself
To unwanted whispers and stares.
The criticism which hurts so much
I know to be unfair.

There are many quick to judge me,
Criticizing without a clue.
But they never offer a shred of help—
They wouldn't know what to do!

The Thing

The Thing is what I turn to
    When you won't obey.
Since this happens frequently,
I use the Thing each day.

It really is hard to know
What Thing I'm going to use.
It all depends, quite frankly,
On what you should abuse.

Detention is one Thing,
Calling home is another.
E-mail allows me quickly
To make a point with mother.

Grades are still another Thing,
And yes, privileges can be yanked.
There's always missed time at recess
Or a parent who could spank.

The Thing can have you missing out
Or being a little late—
To keep you under my control
The Thing can have you wait.

So the Thing is always out there...
I keep it from your view.
But it watches your behavior
And sees everything you do!

Whoopee!

*O*h! It's that time again,
The time of sheer delight!
Area meetings over,
No parents left in sight.

Fund raisers are behind us,
There's money for our school.
Testing has been completed,
We've complied with every rule.

Assemblies were presented,
Outbursts have been but few.
We've managed to enrich the lives
Of all, but one or two.

We've completed the "master" schedule
And noted places to go–
Ordered materials for class next year
Which will help our curriculum grow.

We've taken computer classes
And worked while ill with flu,
Turned in special projects
Our certificates to renew.

But now it's finally over,
And I'm glad for the reprieve.
A few quiet months to myself
Makes me anxious to pack and leave!

CB 22 BD

Finally Summer

M y brain is dead
And I am fed
Up with you
And the things that you do
Driving me mad
And making me glad
That the school year is ending
Hopefully sending
Me
Back to the sea
Where I can be
Blissfully drunk
And hopelessly sunk
In the deep blue abyss
Where I have only one wish:
To remain free from you
And the things that you do!

My Summer

I didn't go to exotic places,
Instead I visited familiar faces.

Spent time with family who live near
And often drank my favorite beer.

I putzed around the house a lot,
Painting endlessly while it was hot.

I spent some time on water clear,
And contemplated on what was dear.

In the afternoon when still light,
I sipped my favorite wine 'til night.

I watched the bats chase fireflies,
Recalling poems that moistened my eyes.

I listened to sounds which are often so rare,
Like the chirping of crickets in warm August air.

I saw my cats dance in neighbors' yards
And played solitaire with an old deck of cards.

But the morning time was always best:
That's when we three would get our rest.

The cats and I would stretch and groan,
As the ceiling fan just hummed and moaned...

Allowing the luxury of silent repose,
Which is time well spent, as everyone knows.

But no matter my travels or where I did go,
Who I did see or how I did grow...

The knowledge that I'm needed here
Is something that I do hold dear.

So the heck with going to exotic places—
I'd rather see familiar faces!

What I Don't Like About Teaching

It's hard to be in the classroom
     When children are out of control.
They are like an angry mob
Once they get on a roll.

I'd rather not be teaching
When their thinking doesn't grow.
I blame myself completely
For the knowledge they don't know.

I hate to be teaching
When I'm called away from class.
This derails my momentum
And thwarts my instructional task!

It's no fun to be instructing
When children don't seem to care.
I'm annoyed when they attempt to challenge
Through action or angry stare.

I dislike being the teacher
When my planning goes astray
By unforeseen occurrences
Which happen from day to day.

I'm overwhelmed with this job of teaching—
There's always too much to do.
It wears me out and casts me off
Like a pair of worn out shoes!

What I Like About Teaching

I love to be in the classroom
With children all around.
Their robust vitality
Keeps me up— not down.

I love when I am teaching
To watch their thinking grow.
I get enthusiastic
When they let their knowledge show.

I love to be a teacher
Exploring relationships in my class.
I'm filled with overwhelming pride
When tests they easily pass.

It's great to be teaching
When I can follow a routine.
I feel a sense of accomplishment
When I've kept the class serene.

It's fun to be a teacher
When everything falls in place.
I love children to have faith in me
Regardless of creed or race.

Yes, I'm proud to be a teacher
Who helps children find their way.
It's simply the very nicest job—
Despite what I sometimes say!

*See the
Child,
Nurture the
Hope...*

Here They Come

At eight fifty-five each morning,
From the silence I do hear,
The sounds of voices far away
Which gradually become quite clear.

They're the children that I work with,
The ones that I adore.
They pour into the classroom
Through the open wooden door.

I'm told of every infraction,
Every naughty thing they see.
I always act completely shocked—
That's what they expect from me.

But I enjoy every morning
And the chaos that they bring.
The tales they tell and tattle
Always make my spirit sing!

For they offer me a treasure,
Which is mine and mine alone.
No queen would possess greater wealth
Should she rule from a golden throne

Yes, a teacher's life is hectic—
Downright hard, many would say.
But the devotion of little children
Always works to save each day!

God's Child

*T*wisting and turning at a maddening pace,
Your look so intense it distorts your face...

Fingers so stiff as they move around,
The things that you spin almost never touch
ground.

Your life is consumed by the oddest of things:
Crumpled up paper which you chew on and fling.

My job is to teach you to prosper and grow,
Maintain a skill which will develop you, so—

There will be meaning to the life that I see.
Twisting and turning—Lord, it could have been
me!

You

I'm always amazed at the things that you do,
　　Like not washing with soap or never tying
　　　　your shoes—

Wearing clothes that are dirty, ragged and ripped,
Elastic so old that pants hang from your hip!

Shoes and old socks in need of the trash,
You valiantly cling to as if they were cash.

Comfort, you stress, is important to you—
I'll keep what is filthy, to heck with the new!

So despite my efforts to turn you around,
You cavort in these clothes as if a stage clown—

Asserting yourself by the things that you wear,
As you drift through each day without even a care!

A Teacher's Duty

I'm worn out with worry, watching your life,
So fraught with danger and internal strife—
Seeking to guide and instruct, as I do,
Knowing I'm useless at managing you.

I don't have your trust—
You've held that back,
Pushed me away,
Now we're way off track.

So, I'm waiting for time to pass, as it will,
Allowing for purpose to once again fill
My life with direction and permit me once more
To summon the courage to open the door...

Which leads to the soul of another lost child,
Withdrawn and abandoned, and incredibly wild.

Recess

*I*t's ten-forty-five:
 Time to play!
I haven't a clue
What to do with this day.

Out on the playground
I watch others swing.
While holding my arm up,
I look for a string.

Something to suck on
Is what I would like...
A dirty old straw
Would be my delight.

Around the playground
I search and I see,
A chewed up old straw—
Oh, this is for me!

So, while others play
With laughter and cheer,
I twiddle my straw
With an absence of fear...

Of what lies ahead
In the future for me.
Like a ship with no rudder,
I flounder at sea.

Free Time

To the playground I must go...
Why I must, I do not know.

Children playing all around,
Swinging, running, sliding down—

Equipment meant for only them.
I am lonely, I have no friends.

And so, when I have time to play,
I walk around in an aimless way—

Waiting for some time to pass,
Until when I am able at last—

To return to the shelter of my room.
Safe within its sacred tomb—

Where I'm protected from what I fear:
All of life, which you hold dear.

Uncertain

*L*ittle child of different race,
With dark brown eyes and
brooding face,
Contemplating what she sees—
Chairs, tables and jingling keys.

What is it that life has brought?
Disappointments never sought,
A way of living so unclear,
Prompting many an unhappy tear.

Never knowing what to do,
Unable to tie the simplest shoe,
Dependent upon others' care,
To brush her teeth or comb her hair.

Oh, tell me what she's to do,
Unable to be like me, or you?

Learning to Grow

Third grade is different:
    You must move from class to class.
Children must be flexible—
It's what they need to pass.

One day a third grade student
Said he wouldn't leave so soon.
Although it was time for class to change,
He stayed in his homeroom.

So I gave a gentle reminder,
And pointed to the door.
"Go with the other children,"
But he stayed rigid to the core.

"Be flexible," I suggested,
Then I let my voice fade.
"But if you can't, I'll understand—
I'll just move you back a grade.

"In second grade there's no pressure,
You stay in the same class.
You never go to another room,
Just cooperate and you'll pass."

Well, he thought about what I told him,
Contemplated what I said,
Then up he got and left the room—
To the class he went ahead.

Later, he said, "I'll be flexible!"
It's something he knew he could do.
If other third graders could handle this,
Then he was confident he could, too!

The Test

A little boy is unprepared
Waiting to take a test.
Mentally he will dare
To be rated with the rest.

Difficulty so profound,
A test that's language-based,
Leaves images incomplete,
A frown upon his face.

As he turns his booklet over
To confront another page,
He complains to me that he is sick...
I see a touch of rage.

"I have a headache, my stomach's sore,
My throat is burning, too.
I hate this test," he stares at me—
"I'm beginning to hate you!

"Why am I asked to do this?
What is it that it proves?
I'm not prepared to work this hard.
Please, I just need to move."

But he's not allowed to get up;
Seated he must stay.
He has this test before him
To finish by today.

He labored for an hour,
Read every problem there,
Squirmed a little in his seat
' Til he finished fair and square.

"Oh, good!" he cried, "It's over!
Thank goodness I am through!
Forget the fact that I'll be back—
To do this again with you!"

The Field Trip

One rainy day a trip was made—
To Jamestown they all went.
Two classes of fourth graders,
On large buses they were sent.

What made this journey so special
Were the boys who made this trip.
Not mature like other kids,
Their behavior was apt to slip.

So long before the sun came up,
Buses left the parking lot
With two young boys and their chaperone,
Whose nerves would later be shot.

This trip down south was a long one,
Taking three hours, maybe more.
For these children it was hard to sit...
They were always about the floor.

They finally arrived in a drizzling rain
Ready for their sight-seeing trip.
But when their chaperone wasn't looking,
The boys gave her the slip!

They were into everything at once,
Wiggling and climbing about.
One ran aboard a ship that was docked,
And made the chaperone shout.

During lunch they jumped around
Bouncing from table to table,
Sampling drinks and sandwiches,
Nibbling where they were able.

Two lollipops they brought back to the bus—
It was the ultimate snack.
While the other children slept going home,
They were active all the way back.

It was a trip to remember—
The boys thought it a lark.
They laughed and tugged and ran around
And certainly left their mark.

But the chaperone thought otherwise—
For her it was no fun.
She remarked when back at school again
"STICK A FORK IN ME, I'M DONE!"

Democrat or Republican?

*F*ourth grade presents some problems,
  As everybody knows.
And here's a little problem,
And this is how it goes:

A little boy in fourth grade
Wanted to protect his neck.
So button-down shirts he religiously wore—
He didn't give a heck.

But these shirts were a little formal,
Standing out like a thumb that's sore.
T-shirts and sweat pants were the casual dress,
Which most other children wore.

But he wouldn't give up his button-down shirt,
He'd wear one everyday.
It protected his neck, so what the heck—
He cared not what others might say.

His stubborn stance persisted
Until election day.
When he came in wearing his button-down shirt,
His teacher finally had her say:

"The election was held yesterday
But your Republican dress still shows.
Why aren't you dressing like a Democrat?
Look! Tee-shirts are what goes!"

He was shocked at his oversight,
And eager to make it right.
What seemed impossible to alter
Changed immediately overnight!

No more dressing like a Republican—
From then on he was casual as ever.
And when asked about his button-down shirt,
To this, he replied, NEVER!

Just Give Me A Chance

*S*tanding in a circle, side by side,
Fingers touching fingers, arms stretched
wide—

Turning in a circle as the others sing,
Hands joining hands, forming a small ring—

This is the class I enjoy most of all;
No judgments are made, it's okay if I fall.

The movements I see other children perform
Make me try very hard to be just like the norm.

But I cannot do all the skills that I see;
It's often confusing and frustrating for me.

Moving my body to a rhythmic beat
Is like walking a line with two left feet!

But all that aside, I so love to try.
I seek attention, no longer shy...

Lifting my fingers in a small wave,
Learning to sing and to move and to play...

Coming together for our music class,
Everyone happy and eager to pass!

The PB&J Mystery

*Y*ou were just a child of eight
And had no solid speech.
Dilemmas you were faced with
Presented problems out of reach.

A peanut butter and jelly sandwich
Is one that comes to mind.
You had this sandwich daily,
It was there for you to find.

You didn't want that sandwich,
But there it lay in wait—
Eager for your fingers
To send it to its fate!

So faced with thirty minutes
Of not knowing what to do,
You squeezed that jellied sandwich...
On the floor it turned to glue!

But the hostess saw the jelly,
And the custodian, well, she got mad.
Now you looked for something else to do
With the sandwich that you had.

So out of desperation
You rubbed it back and forth.
Upon the sturdy table legs
It was found both south and north!

We now know why this happened
For your closest friend did mutter:
"He wants a different kind of lunch—
He don't like peanut butter!"

Not Again

*O*nce there was a little boy
   Who had to take a pill.
He did this every day at noon,
He did this with good will.

He'd walk to the nurse's station—
This routine he did each day,
Sign in and state his name and room,
All done the exact same way.

He understood just what to do,
Having mastered this routine.
All was very predictable,
If it stayed the way it seemed.

Then one day no nurse was there,
So he practiced what he knew.
He waited very patiently,
Unsure of what to do.

Then someone else came in the room,
A secretary he had known.
She was prepared to give the pill—
"Oh no!" she heard him groan.

The secretary was not the nurse,
The routine was not the same.
He feared to relearn what he already knew—
So the secretary took the blame.

For the routine had been hard to remember
In its order and detail.
To change the person with the pill
Was just asking him to fail.

Faced with something new to learn,
He really couldn't stand it.
So when the secretary gave him the pill,
She heard him holler, "Damn it!"

Pancake Palace

*O*n Fridays we'd go shopping—
Away from school we'd head.
We had a favorite restaurant;
It was there that we'd get fed.

"I'd like to order pancakes,"
Each child would softly mutter.
But when you ordered you cried out,
"NO SYRUP AND NO BUTTER!"

One morning after getting up,
Your parents planned a treat.
They offered you some pancakes...
"No pancakes!" they heard you shriek.

Mom and Dad were puzzled—
Oh, what were they to think?
Your teacher said you loved these,
But now you think they stink!

While at school you'd learned a lesson—
Life taught you simply this:
To compromise what you despise
So a trip you'd never miss.

The restaurant is what you savored
And though pancakes weren't your thing,
You got to give the orders—
In that restaurant you were king!

The Officer

*Y*ou are a special child to me,
  You police the other kids.
Watching them for every mistake,
Then reporting on what they did.

Detention, you are quick to say,
Is where they need to go.
You taunt them like an older sib,
'Til their tempers start to show.

Then back you come reporting
On something else you've heard—
Stirring up the chaos,
Repeating every word.

Your finger shakes emphatically
As you put each child in place.
But I must remain quite serious
And hide laughter in my face.

Yes, you are a little dickens
With your fussy, meddling touch.
But when your time with me is through
I'll miss you oh so much!

The Assignment

Writing poems makes me want to fight;
They're hard to read and hard to write.

I would rather play all day,
To heck with what my teacher will say.

But if I don't, I know she'll fuss;
I might even miss my bus!

So I've decided to write just one,
Even though I'd rather write none!

Suspended In Space

What do I do? What do I do?

I have no idea, so I'll just stare at you!

If I stare long enough, maybe you'll know

How lonely I am—perhaps it will show.

So I'll sit on this bench, with no clue what to do,

Staring straight ahead, looking directly at you.

Where's Wallace?

Wallace is a little child
  In love with Dr. Seuss.
He frantically looks for him
Whenever he gets loose.

He cherishes those books of his
And tries to take them home.
He looks for them in classrooms,
So throughout the school he'll roam.

Wallace has a favorite place
Where he can be found.
He's in the school library,
Usually face down—

Hiding his precious quarry.
Raise him up and you will find
Dr. Seuss's wonderful animal friends
Of every make and kind.

So if not watched every minute,
He'll quickly run about,
Speed off to the library,
And then he won't come out.

He'll disturb the librarian
Who's quiet and sedate.
Working to put books away—
A job that keeps her late.

He'll gather every Seuss book,
While keeping you at bay.
Then pretend his hands are empty
As he tries to get away.

He's recognized easily
And known for getting loose.
But to me he'll be remembered
As the boy who loves Dr. Seuss!

The Pinch

$\mathcal{I}$t happened one afternoon,
  It happened kind of late.
It happened to the nicest man—
It was to be his fate.

He was entering the classroom
While Wallace was running out.
To the library Wallace was headed—
"Seuss! Seuss!" we heard him shout!

"What's going on?" the man questioned
As he stopped Wallace from running away.
But angered that he couldn't leave
Wallace speared him in the doorway.

The poor man saw this coming,
On his toes he quickly got.
But pinned by the door he couldn't move,
So his stomach took the shot.

"He got me!" he cried out in pain.
"My stomach won't be the same!
Why did I have to come in just then?"
We heard him softly exclaim.

So in pain the man left the doorway.
He had kept Wallace from getting loose.
But a little voice kept pleading,
"Dr. Seuss, Dr. Seuss, Dr. Seuss!"

The Tragedy

I show anger wherever I go,
At you, at me, at people I know.

I want to be happy like the children I see,
But life is not fair, it cheated me.

All that I have is here on the floor,
Beat up old sneakers that keep my feet sore.

A ragged old backpack I take where I go.
It holds some old stuff, but what, I don't know.

My home keeps me warm but offers little more;
Since I haven't a bed I must sleep on the floor.

In a tattered old sleeping bag my body will lay,
Preparing for battles with the coming of day.

Content for the night I drift off to sleep.
Tears moisten my pillow— I quietly weep.

Drowning

I got mad and pinched your arm,
    But now I must obey.
I have to type an essay
And complete it all today.

You've taken me to The Office;
I've been removed from class.
I failed to cooperate with you,
And decided to harass.

So to a room I am led–
At a desk I must sit
I must type on an Alpha Smart—
And this, I cannot quit!

But like a boy who's drowning,
I'll find someone to nab.
Now that I am all alone,
A secretary I'll grab!

I'll get up in just a minute,
And to her desk I'll go,
Stand nearby and question her
For answers I already know.

I'll cling and cling and cling to her
And make her really mad!
Then when she shows she's angry,
I'll make my face look sad.

I'm drowning in bad behavior,
And I'll grasp whoever is near.
I'm struggling hard to understand—
At times, there's much I fear.

So please don't ever leave me,
Even though I can annoy.
I'm frightened of being left alone...
I'm just a little boy!

Please Don't Tell Mother

*P*lease don't tell mother
　About what I did today.

Please don't tell mother
That I lost time at play.

Please don't tell mother
That I talked back in class.

Please don't tell mother
That I choose to give you sass.

Please don't tell mother
That I wouldn't cooperate

Please don't tell mother
That for lunch I was so late

Please don't tell mother
That while upset, I pinched your arm.

Please don't tell mother
That I caused other children harm.

Please don't tell mother
I promise I'll obey.

All I really want to do
Is have fun at school and play.

Please do tell mother
That I love to be in school,

Even though most every day
I break most every rule!

You Don't Care

*Y*ou're big and lazy and you don't care,
   Your dirty fingerprints are everywhere—

Hair a mess, chocolate on your face,
Clothes too big that fall from your waist—

You disrupt others and do as you please,
Close down options with apparent ease—

Oblivious to hardships heading your way,
Unprepared for living and the ensuing days—

When your life will be governed by others,
                not me,
And the decisions you've made will be the
                prison you see!

Me First

hanging my mind is frustrating for you—
But why are you angry, what did I do?

Because I don't listen, because I don't care...
What difference does it make?

To me life's unfair!

I have nothing to lose, so a problem I'll be—
Showing my anger is what I want you to see.

The resentment and rage that dwells in my life
Has severed my hope like a swiftly thrown knife.

Afraid

*A*ngry little Albert
    Faces life each day
Ready to do battle
With everything you say.

Eager to be independent,
Anxious to be on the move,
Pushing others to one side,
Quick to get in his groove...

Vicious when confronted,
Teeth bearing down,
Hands pinching and grabbing,
Kicking all around.

I'll strike out if I'm thwarted!
Albert silently vows to do.
Your rules are meant for others—
WATCH OUT! I could hurt you!

My life is very lonely;
Others are afraid of me.
I never show my sweetness
And the child I long to be.

So I come to school each morning
Plotting trouble that's taboo—
Paying no attention
To what Teacher says to do.

I'm always into mischief,
Other children's books and food,
Running into classrooms,
Disrupting Teacher's mood...

Causing havoc and disturbance,
Screaming when called down,
Unable to speak my frustration
I tantrum on the ground...

For my life is very empty—
I allow few people in.
Trust is something I can't do
'Cause then I couldn't win.

But what thwarts my teacher most
Is my need to take command.
I cannot put my faith in her...
Yet I long to understand.

Lost and Alone

A troubled mind I see each day,
Such confused thinking makes me
turn away.
Mindless hitting and aggressive acts
Displays your anger and what your life lacks.

But to me you come every morning at eight,
Never ever tardy, never ever late.
I am your teacher, to my class you're assigned;
I must teach you something, expand your mind.

But mental health I know little about;
Without proper training, I'm stumbling about.
Watching you think, like leaves in the wind,
Your mind so flaccid that it yields and bends...

To wayward ideas and lies that you tell.
You're often convincing, but many know well
Of the severe psychosis which lingers within,
Corrupting your childhood from what should
have been.

I ache for your suffering, for it's obvious to me
That your needs are great. Yet no one else sees
The haunted child with the far away eyes,
Ensnared in his web of deception and lies!

Unprepared

*P*oor little Bobby
    Sits quietly in class,
Never knowing what to do,
Hands appearing clasped—
Unsure of what's expected,
Withdrawn and alone.

Parents lament daily,
While talking on the phone,
Angry with each other
For this child of theirs at home
Is often left unsupervised
And allowed to freely roam.

At school he sits quietly,
Though efforts are always made
To encourage his thinking,
Which must be nurtured and be saved.
But thoughts must be cared for
As they germinate and grow..

For if a mind is left unchallenged,
Then the absence of thought will show
In a lack of love and interest
For what is bright and new...
Leaving a child like Bobby
Unprepared for what to do.

You Won't Get Away

You're not going to get away
   By pretending not to know.
I'm aware that you're capable
By everything you show.

Don't hide behind confusion;
That's only subterfuge.
A trick you learned long ago
Is now a thing you use.

Don't pretend that you don't get it,
Or say you don't understand.
Don't waste your time on antics,
Or push me away with your hand.

Don't constantly talk or interrupt;
You know that isn't right.
I plan to hold you accountable
Should we stay here half the night!

Don't be so uncontrollable,
Causing disturbances at will.
It's wrong to lose self-control;
You have assignments to fulfill!

At school you'll learn of choices,
And important ones to make.
Good habits bring their own rewards—
Bad ones, we'll have to break.

You see, I won't let you get away
And waste more precious time.
The fact that people allowed this at all,
To me,— is an unspeakable crime!

School–
The Heart
of the
Matter

The School Secretary

*W*hat I do is amazing to me:
Under pressure I type with lightening
speed.

Coffee in hand, I hurry and dial,
To determine the whereabouts of a small tardy
child.

Without losing a beat, I take lists from my desk,
Type names, dates and grades without pausing
to rest.

As I start to wind down, my energy drops,
Then in comes the mail to be sorted and boxed.

When someone is sick, the stress really starts.
With ragged nerves I move like a dart—

From phones, to computers, then back to my desk.
No job could be harder; it's the ultimate test.

But when the day is over, and all is done,
I'd rather this job— it is second to none!

Where's the Nurse?

A nurse is very important.
    She ministers to kids each day,
Taking care of accidents
Which happen during play.

She often checks for head lice
And cleans up after kids who heave.
She calls doctors about ringworm
And gets sick children ready to leave.

She reports a variety of accidents
And takes care of blood and gore.
She dispenses loads of Ritalin
To the multitude who come through the door.

She hands out ice bags a plenty
And checks for eyes that cannot see.
So if Trisha leaves who'll help us?
She says, "It won't be me!"

She's leaving to take it easy
And relax while at the beach.
This is a wonderful place for Trish—
'Cause she wants to stay out of reach!

So as the clinic door closes,
Her memory will stay behind.
We'll call it into duty
If a substitute we can't find!

The Enforcer

We have a special person,
    She's a teacher at our school—
In charge of detention,
Enforcer of every rule.

We call her when she's needed
For anger or for sass.
If you make a bad decision,
You'll sit with her in class.

She has a dark red notebook,
In her desk it always stays.
She keeps a daily record
Of names and times and days.

She bustles in our classroom
With her hands upon her hips.
"What is going on? she asks
And she tightens up her lips.

No child escapes her scrutiny
Or gets anything by.
This teacher is a super sleuth
With a very piercing eye.

But those of us who know her,
Know the kindness in her heart,
And accept this role she handles...
Like an actor, she plays a part!

The Master

*L*inda's a master teacher,
    Ordered and precise.
She keeps her room immaculate
And all her records nice!

Documents are readable,
Her results are always fine.
No response is ever late,
She keeps her dates in line.

Custodians are in awe of her—
They never fail to say
How clean and neat her room is kept
At the end of every day.

Sprays and cleaners are always there
For her daily use.
She wipes away the smudge and sludge
From children's constant abuse.

She's quite neat about herself, you know,
And protects those dainty fingers,
Keeping her hand in plastic wrap
While over her sandwich, she lingers.

She knows about computers,
And screening issues, too.
I don't believe there really is
Too much our Linda can't do.

She's structured and she's orderly,
She's dropped off at school by eight.
She's picked up promptly at three forty-five—
And Linda's never late!

She's retiring to Florida,
A life of bliss and pleasure.
But the master's shoes shall not be filled...
To that, no one can measure!

Mr. Gym

We had a wonderful teacher,
    He taught every child in school.
He emphasized values and principles,
And P.E. was his tool.

In kindergarten he often scolded,
Don't be unkind to your friends.
He wanted to encourage fellowship—
This is where friendship first begins.

In first grade he introduced teamwork—
Learning to support each other.
He stressed we're all related
Like a sister to a brother.

In second grade he spoke of tolerance
For children who're less able.
He set a place for every child
Like a father heading a table.

In third grade he stressed fairness—
Cheating was never allowed.
If he felt someone was going astray,
Then he raised his voice quite loud.

The fourth grade he saw differently—
He wanted their love and respect.
So he played with them quite often,
And for this they hugged his neck.

The fifth grade wanted to be recognized
For what they had learned and done.
So he challenged them to perform—
Their admiration he'd already won.

The sixth grade had put it together—
Their lessons were now complete.
As rising middle schoolers
He was confident they could compete.

Yes, he had given each child a treasure,
The gift of showing he cared.
And that's why each will reach farther—
Perhaps more than anyone dared!

The Octopus

*S*he's just a hard worker
    Who often stays late—
She handles far too many jobs
And does them all first rate.

She heads a weekly committee
Bringing issues to the table.
She's in charge of lengthy paper trails
Updating children's labels.

She's responsible for testing
And filling out various forms,
Preparing extensive documents
Which check test scores against norms.

She conducts parent meetings
And offers good advice,
Keeps the staff well informed
Through records so precise.

She commutes just like a postman
Through rain, sleet and snow—
Then assumes a duty station
Before the buses show.

She also runs a classroom
Teaching children who are less able.
And, Oh! did I forget to say
She educates the disabled?

And this is just her day job—
She has a family, too.
So after leaving the classroom
There's still more for her to do!

She needs to have more time to plan
And organize her day—
But duties and obligations
Offer no leeway.

If planning and organization
As priorities are kept low,
Then teaching becomes nothing more
Than fast food on the go.

So if you're serious about teaching,
Then help her do her job.
Don't expect her to do everything
While her time and energy you rob.

Their Champion

We have a music teacher
    Who we believe to be the best!
She charges through activities
And never stops to rest.

She works with Monday chorus
Planning many a wondrous thing.
Often accepting children
Who hardly know how to sing.

But being a member of chorus
Builds self-esteem in school.
So she'll accept you into this grouping—
Provided you follow all her rules!

She counts you in, and looks inside,
And finds what you do well.
Then shows you off at assemblies
And says you're doing swell!

She's simply a fabulous lady
Who has talent and insight.
We rely on her for courage
To do what she knows is right.

What Have We Learned?

The Purpose of Education

Children come each day to schools
    to learn to live by many rules.
Conforming is the task at hand—
A lesson taught in many lands.

Lining up against a wall,
Walking quietly in a hall,
Following teachers to and fro...
Obedience each child must know.

Pledging allegiance is what we express,
'Tis a rule we all address.
Carrying flags and banners high...
Many children don't know why.

But is there something larger here,
Something that we all hold dear,
Values that we know are true,
Integrity living in me and you?

Is this the lesson we need to stress,
Regardless of culture or manner of dress?
Seeking understanding which unites us all,
Allowing each person to stand up tall...

Secure in their truth and what they know,
Offering to others so they may grow
And benefit from wisdom true...
The kind that lives in me and you.

A Child's Spirit

What is the spirit of living?
How does it come about?
Does it always stay in the same spot?
Or is it ever allowed to come out?

Where is the spirit of a small child?
Is it beneath a smile that it hides?
Or does it lurk behind a knowing glance?
Is this where it resides?

Does it travel down from Heaven's Gate
To comfort and protect?
Does it rest upon a pillow
Just below a child's small neck?

Can we recognize spirits
In the children we teach each day?
Can we seek their special guidance
To help learning along its way?

Are there little spirit angels
Who inhabit this planet Earth?
Here to promote our tolerance,
Understanding and self-worth?

Does the act of teaching,
Which we eagerly impart,
Shape the little spirit
And direct its tiny heart?

C3 88 80

The Cushion

What makes a school a good fit
For each child in attendance there?
Is it the building or books we see?
Or is it a quality rare?

I believe it is in the cushion,
The caring professionals at school,
Who absorb a child's imperfections—
All done as an unspoken rule.

Without a cushion to offer support,
School can be a horrible fit.
Having to go every day to this place
Can promote the desire to quit.

It's important to take notice of teachers
And see how they compare.
Watch for kindness among them,
Seek those who are honest and fair.

Give your child a fighting chance,
Give them a supportive school.
Make sure the cushion is firmly in place,
Make this your number one rule!

Feed The Children

A chef who works in a kitchen,
Preparing a gourmet feast,
Requires the best ingredients—
Leftovers won't do in the least.

He'll plan what to fix quite completely,
Pay attention to every detail,
Organize just what to serve—
Then see that his meal doesn't fail.

The reason his feast is successful
Is because all his plans are first rate;
Taking the time, and working with care,
Puts quality food on his plate.

And just like a chef in a kitchen,
A teacher has much to prepare.
Lessons require lots of planning
To reach children who often don't care.

But left without preparation time,
A good teacher cannot create.
The gourmet meal our children deserve
Will sadly be missed from their plate.

So if fine dining is promised
By administrators in control,
Then they must allow the time to prepare,
For a meal that's not half, but whole.

Remember the chef in the kitchen,
Who takes care of every detail.
Give your teachers the time that they need,
So their efforts to teach will not fail.

The Big Game

After you learn about a game,
You'll gather kids to play.
They'll spend much time upon the field
And practice hard each day.

They'll learn to bring equipment,
Find the positions they must take,
Memorize the rules they'll need—
And try never to be late.

But the truth is many children
Who daily come to school,
Will never make the game on time
And will never learn the rules.

They'll forget all their equipment
And the positions that they'll play.
They'll often become discouraged
Despite what you might say.

But at least they know there is a game
And they know where they must go.
So it doesn't really matter
'Cause eventually they'll show.

So let's take those children,
The ones who lag behind,
Put them on a different team
And let their knowledge shine.

Let them head a separate group
Of kids who just don't know
What the game is all about
Or where they need to go.

This process is called mainstreaming—
But it's sort of in reverse.
You take the kids who lag behind
And now you put them first.

Let them be the leaders—
For once, put them in charge!
Shore up their sagging self-esteem
Into something grand and large.

Yes, teach all children together...
But assign each child a place.
Then value their contribution...
Insure a smile upon each face!

Where's the Rest of the Train?

A teacher is like an engine,
    A powerful driving force,
Who directs the flow of instruction
By setting the educational course.

She maps out where she's going,
Provisions with materials she'll need,
Prepares for classroom discussion
And encourages each child to read.

So who's to help the unsure child,
The one who's far behind?
How should we address his needs?
What methods should we keep in mind?

If the teacher empowers the classroom,
Then she's pulling a lot of weight.
Why not have an instructional assistant
Help the children who are conceptually late?

Then have a special ed teacher
At each grade level to create
Lessons for the disabled child,
So progress they, too, can make.

Teach all children in the same classroom,
But acknowledge what each group needs.
Consider other instructional models—
Please...won't someone take the lead?

The Puzzle

*L*ife can be puzzling,
Of that there's no doubt.
Finding your place
Is what life's all about!

But to find your place
You must see how things fit,
Observe how things work,
Then learn where to sit.

Putting puzzles together
Will help a child see
How pieces connect
To form what's to be.

Playing with puzzles
Will naturally show
That each piece has a place,
Which a child will soon know.

And just like a puzzle
Our children will see
How they fit with others
And where they need to be!

Show and Tell

We all remember show and tell
   And how exciting it was to share.
But it need not be a thing of the past...
We can do it any time, anywhere!

So in the spirit of giving,
Let's remember those days gone by.
Recapture some of what we've lost—
Let's start right now and try!

While you're on vacation
Look for something that's unique...
A video, book or artifact,
Something a teacher might seek.

Put history back in the classroom
Through items brought to school.
Children love to see new things—
To them, the unusual is cool!

Expose all children to knowledge,
Bring back a treasure to share.
Let them benefit from where you've been,
Send the message, "Yes, I care!"

It's Up to You

*E*very year universities strive
To collect donations through pledges
and drives.

This money they use to expand and grow—
They accomplish much; it's quick to show!

So let's employ this method with elementary
schools—
Use pledges and drives as additional tools...

To increase the budgets of educational needs—
For enrichment programs need funds to
succeed,

(Little children depend on us,
So this plan we must discuss.)

Write a check for a dollar or two;
Remember, it goes for something new!

Prepare your envelope with a check to send
Addressed to the school you used to attend.

Then rest assured what you did was right;
Turn in for bed and have a good night!

CB 97 BO

Do We Dare?

*R*equirements are important,
They allow us entrance in.
They qualify us for what we seek
And allow us all to win.

They are necessary and important
And what we rely upon.
They help to move things speedily
And allow us to carry on.

So let us look at the function
Of the elementary schools we use.
Should we have entrance requirements
To keep classrooms from being misused?

Should disruption be handled elsewhere
If it's chronic and prolonged?
Would this change be useful...
Even if some thought it...wrong?

Should we have readiness expectations
That require self control?
Keeping distractions to a minimum—
Should this be our goal?

Would this plan offer quality instruction
To every child in its care?
Should we proceed with this discussion,
Or...do we dare?

The Huddle

A winning team has great coaching,
  They know which plays will work.
They're quick to send in resources
Depending where a need may lurk.

A school board makes up a coaching staff—
They direct resources to our schools.
They prioritize the needs they see
And are often unfairly ridiculed.

So let's look at the election process
And have each candidate spend a week or two
In a grade level they'd like to represent,
Seeing issues from a different point of view.

Then they'll be prepared when people speak
With the understanding that they've gained.
This will familiarize them with a variety of concerns
And can't help but improve their campaign!

With twelve members on the school board,
Each official will represent
The issues unique to the grades in their care—
This will help to make voters content!

It's the link which has been needed
Telling us which member to address.
With so many issues requiring attention,
This approach offers direct access.

Cast Upon the Shore

Where do teachers often go
    When cast upon the shore?
Battered by the endless tide
Of children at the door?

They've waited on the beaches
Building castles made of sand...
But when the tide gets through with them
What they've built no longer stands.

Yes, they accept this job with fortitude,
Courage and true might.
But the tide exacts a terrible toll
And devastates overnight.

Still, the weary teachers brave the tide
And are pummeled by the surf.
Tides are unpredictable,
Eroding their self-worth.

But teachers stumble back to shore
To take again their place.
Having built another castle,
The tide they will embrace.

Yet, on some rare occasions,
A hurricane comes in.
Its strength is so mighty,
It's useless to defend.

A hurricane of children
Is a moving, powerful force,
Which crushes many a teacher
Despite their instructional course.

It can leave our finest teachers
In a wasted, broken state.
Their identity lies in ruin—
Here rests their daily fate!

With their noble natures weakened,
Unable to build anymore,
They pick up their splintered spirit
And walk quietly down the shore.

A Teacher's Dream

I f all things were possible
 and wishes could come true,
Here would be my special list—
I'll share it all with you.

I'd seek a climate of sensitivity
With plenty of time to teach.
Paperwork would be prioritized low
And placed within another's reach.

Resources would be abundant,
There would always be books to spare,
And people taking interest in children—
With knowledge and skills to share.

There would be mentoring for new teachers
Who sometimes need to be braced.
We'd give them the wisdom of experience
To help them while in the workplace.

We'd schedule time for collaboration,
Acknowledge the need to compare,
Correlate lessons taught with each other—
And ideas and materials we'd share.

We'd restore teacher authority
And handle discipline within our rooms.
We'd regain the influence that once we had —
A place of honor we'd resume.

We'd also consider something new
To help during times of stress.
Testing times or when projects are due
Is when there's lots of unrest.

Yes, we'd have a new sort of employee
Who is hired for a week or two.
They'd help out during our busy times
Doing whatever they are asked to do.

Retirees would love this!
They could easily plan their days.
Knowing what to expect in a job
Would save them from the substitute maze.

And lastly, for the career teachers,
Who really just need a break,
We'd rotate them to a related job
So teaching they'd never forsake.

In my dream we'd all come together
In an effort to make things fit.
To this goal we'd work tirelessly—
And we'd never think to quit.

Yes, I've thought about this often,
So I'll plant this tiny seed,
Water it with my daily prayers—
And ask God to let it succeed!

A Child's Prayer

L ittle angel that dwells within,
  Seeking always to be my friend—

Favor me with love and grace,
And keep a smile upon my face.

Shelter me from stormy night,
Keep my eyes upon thy light...

Until my life will come to pass
And I will be at home at last...

Safe with those whose love I share,
Free from worry, free from care.

See the Child,
Nurture the Hope